Betty Head
Presented to:

Robert & JoANN Flint
By:

Hannah Whitall Smith

SELECTIONS FROM
*The God of
All Comfort*

Perfect
Peace

MOODY PRESS
CHICAGO

All Scripture, unless indicated, are taken from the New King James Version. Copyright © 1979, 1980, 1982 by Thomas Nelson, Inc. Used by permission. All rights reserved.

Scripture quotations marked (NIV) are taken from the *Holy Bible: New International Version*. Copyright © 1973, 1978, 1984 International Bible Society.
Used by permission of Zondervan Publishing House. All rights reserved.

Editorial services: Julie-Allyson Ieron, Joy Media

Design: Ragont Design, Barrington, IL.

Photography Credits:
Corbis: cover, pages 3, 16-25, 30, 38-51, 58-63, 70, 76, 84-87, 92-95
Photodisc: cover, pages 5-14, 26-30, 32-36, 46, 52-57, 64-75, 78-83, 86, 88-91

———— ISBN: 0-8024-6692-3

1 3 5 7 9 10 8 6 4 2

$\mathcal{T}$ABLE OF CONTENTS

SECTION ONE   7
The Source of All Comfort

SECTION TWO   17
God's Name

SECTION THREE   57
A Matter of Faith

SECTION FOUR   85
Christ in Us, the Hope of Glory

SECTION ONE

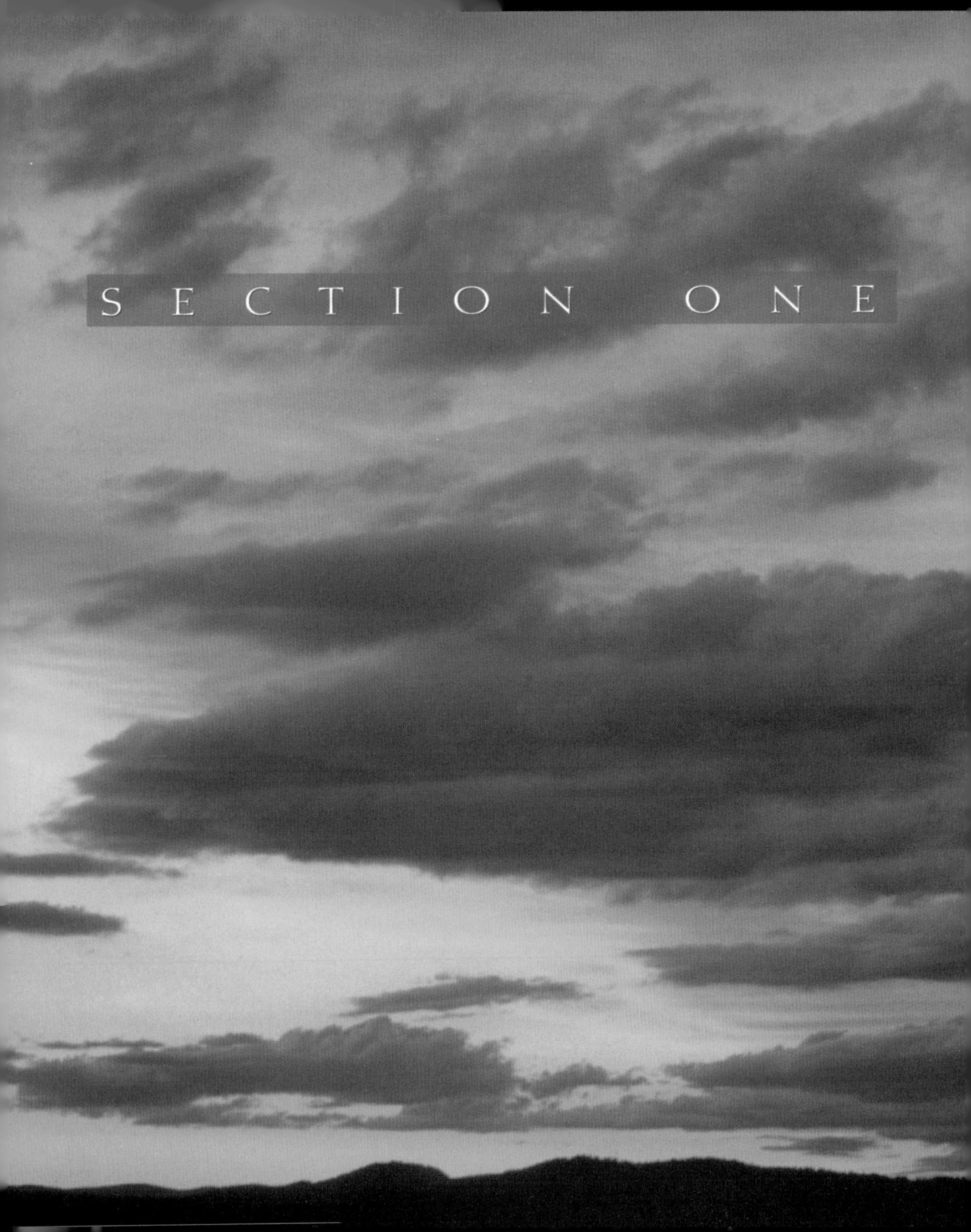

The
Source of
All Comfort

Plenty of outward discomforts there may be, and many earthly sorrows and trials, but through them all the soul that knows God cannot but dwell inwardly in a fortress of perfect peace.

Perfect peace

That deep and lasting peace and comfort of soul, which nothing earthly can disturb, and which is declared to be the portion of those who embrace it, comes only from the Lord Jesus Christ. As we seek to avail ourselves of it, there is God's part in the matter and there is our part. God's part is always to run after us. Christ came to seek and to save that which was lost. This is always the divine part; but too often we do not understand it. We think that the Lord is the One who is lost, and that our part is to seek and find Him.

Because we do not know Him, we naturally get all sorts of wrong ideas about Him. We think He is an angry Judge who is on the watch for our slightest faults, or a harsh Taskmaster determined to exact from us the uttermost service, or a self-absorbed Deity demanding His full measure of honor and glory, or a far-off Sovereign concerned only with His own affairs and indifferent to our welfare.

Who can wonder that such a God can neither be loved nor trusted?

But it is impossible for anyone who really knows God to have such uncomfortable thoughts about Him.

If we would really hear God and believe what we hear, He cannot do other than care for us as He cares for the apple of His eye; and all that tender love and divine wisdom can do for our welfare He will unfailingly do.

Not a single loophole or worry or fear is left to the soul that knows God.

You will keep him in perfect peace, whose mind is stayed on You, because he trusts in You. Trust in the Lord forever, for in the Lord is everlasting strength

(ISAIAH 26:3–4).

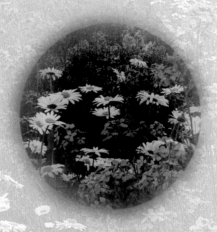

How am I to get to know Him? you ask. Other people seem to have some kind of inward revelation that makes them know Him, but no matter how much I pray, everything seems dark to me. I want to know God, but I do not see how to manage it.

When I refer to "knowing God," I do not mean any mystical interior revelations of any kind. Such revelations are delightful when you can have them, but they are not always at your command. The kind of knowing I mean is the plain, matter-of-fact knowledge of God's nature and character that comes to us by believing what is revealed in the Bible concerning Him.

I mean, to be practical, that when I read in the Bible that God is love, I am to believe it, just because it is written and not because I have had any inward revelation that it is true; and when the Bible says that He cares for us as He cares for the lilies of the field and the birds of the air, I am to believe it, just because it is written. The Bible is a statement, not of theories, but of actual facts.

Things are not true because they are in the Bible, but they are only in the Bible because they are true.

SECTION TWO

God's
Name

Then Moses said to God, "Indeed, when I come to the children of Israel and say to them, 'The God of your fathers has sent me to you,' and they say to me, 'What is His name?' what shall I say to them?"

And God said to Moses, "I AM WHO I AM." And He said, "Thus you shall say to the children of Israel, 'I AM has sent me to you'" (EXODUS 3:13–14).

Everything in a universe will depend upon the sort of creator and ruler who has brought that universe into existence; the whole welfare of the human beings who have been placed there is of necessity bound up with the character of their Creator. If the God who created us is a good God, then everything must of necessity be all right for us, since a good God cannot ordain any but good things. But if He is a bad God, or a careless God, or an unkind God, then we cannot be sure that anything is right, and can have no peace or comfort anywhere.

Therefore, we need first of all to find out what is His name, or, in other words, what is His character.

In the book of Revelation He declares: "'I am the Alpha and the Omega, the Beginning and the End,' says the Lord, 'who is and who was and who is to come, the Almighty'"

"I am the Alpha

(Revelation 1:8). The simple words "I am" express eternity and unchange-ableness, which is the first element necessary in a God who is to be depended upon. No dependence could be placed upon a changeable God. He must be the same yesterday, today, and forever if we are to have any peace or comfort.

and Omega"

God tells us through all the pages of His Book what He is. "I am," He says, "all that my people need": "I am their strength"; "I am their wisdom"; "I am their righteousness"; "I am their peace"; "I am their salvation"; "I am their life"; "I am their all in all."

If we would know the length, and breadth, and height, and depth of what God meant when He gave to Moses that apparently unfinished name of "I am," we shall find it revealed in Christ. He and He alone is the translation of God. He and He alone is the image of the invisible God.

No other witness but Christ can tell us of the real secrets of God's bosom, for of none other can it be said, as it is of Him, that "the only begotten Son who is in the bosom of the Father, he hath declared him." It will make all the difference between comfort and discomfort in our Christian lives, whether or not we believe this to be a fact.

No matter what my own thoughts and feelings are, nor what anybody else may say, I know that what Christ says about God must be true, for He knew, and nobody else does, and I am going to believe Him right straight through, come what may.

"I am their

peace"

Praise be to the God and Father of our Lord Jesus Christ, the Father of compassion and the God of all comfort, who comforts us in all our troubles, so that we can comfort those in any trouble with the comfort we ourselves have received from God (2 CORINTHIANS 1:3–4 NIV).

Among all the names that reveal God, the "God of all comfort," is one of the loveliest and most comforting. However full of discomforts the outward life of the followers of such a God might be, their inward life must be under all circumstances a comfortable life.

The God

of all comfort

The reality of being comforted seems to me almost more delightful than any other thing in life. When as little children we have cuddled up into our mother's lap after a fall or a misfortune, and have felt her dear arms around us, and her soft kisses on our hair, we have had comfort. When, as grown-up people, after a hard day's work, we have put on our slippers and seated ourselves by the fire, in an easy chair with a book, we have had comfort. When someone whom we dearly love has been ill almost unto death, and has been restored to us in health again, we have had comfort.

He is the "God who comforts the downcast" (2 Corinthians 7:6); it is just because you are downcast that you can claim the comforting of Christ. The psalmist tells us that God will "comfort [us] on every side" (Psalm 71:21), and what an all-embracing bit of comfort this is. "On every side," no aching spot to be left uncomforted.

The "God of all comfort" sent His Son to be the Comforter of a mourning world.

Our Comforter is close at hand. He abides with us. He declared, "Peace I leave with you, My peace I give to you; not as the world gives do I give to you. Let not your heart be troubled, neither let it be afraid" (John 14:27).

How can we, in the face of these tender and loving words, go about with troubled and frightened hearts? God's comfort is being continually and abundantly given, but unless you will accept it you cannot have it. In this matter of comfort it is exactly as it is in every other experience in the religious life. God says, "Believe, and then you can feel."

If we want to be comforted, we must make up our minds to believe every word of comfort God has ever spoken; and we must refuse to listen to any words of discomfort spoken by our own hearts or our circumstances.

He leads me

The Lord is my shepherd; I shall not want"
(Psalm 23:1). With the Lord for our Shepherd,
all that this psalm promises must be ours, and we
will be able to say with truimph: "Surely
goodness and mercy shall follow me [pursue,
overtake] all the days of my life, and I will
dwell in the house of the Lord forever."

beside the still waters

PSALM 23

The Lord is my shepherd; I shall not want.

He makes me to lie down in green pastures; He leads me beside the still waters.

He restores my soul; He leads me in the paths of righteousness for His name's sake.

Yea, though I walk through the valley of the shadow of death, I will fear no evil; for You are with me; Your rod and Your staff, they comfort me.

You prepare a table before me in the presence of my enemies; You anoint my head with oil; my cup runs over.

Surely goodness and mercy shall follow me all the days of my life; and I will dwell in the house of the Lord forever.

Perhaps no aspect in which the Lord reveals Himself to us is fuller of genuine comfort than the aspect set forth in the Twenty-third Psalm, and in its corresponding passage in the tenth chapter of John. The psalmist tells me that the Lord is my Shepherd, and the Lord Himself declares that He is the good Shepherd. Can we conceive of anything more comforting?

The Lord God of heaven and earth, the almighty Creator of all things, He who holds the universe in His hand as though it were a very little thing, He is your Shepherd, and has charged Himself with the care and keeping of you, as a shepherd is charged with the care and keeping of his sheep.

Say the words over to yourself with all the willpower you can muster, "The Lord is my Shepherd. He is. He is. No matter what I feel, He says He is, and He is. I am going to believe it, come what may."

What shall you do to make Christ your Savior? Every soul that will begin from today believing in the Good Shepherd and trusting itself to His care finds itself feeding in His green pastures, and walking beside His still waters.

Trust and follow your Shepherd now and here. Abandon yourself to His care and guidance, and trust Him utterly.

The Lord

is my Shepherd

The Lord's Prayer
MATTHEW 6:9–13

"Our Father in heaven, hallowed be Your name. Your kingdom come. Your will be done on earth as it is in heaven. Give us this day our daily bread. And forgive us our debts, as we forgive our debtors. And do not lead us into temptation, but deliver us from the evil one. For Yours is the kingdom and the power and the glory forever. Amen."

One of the most illuminating names of God is the one revealed by our Lord Jesus Christ—the name of Father. While God had been called throughout the ages by many other names that express other aspects of His character, Christ alone revealed Him to us under the all-inclusive name of Father—a name that holds within itself all other names of wisdom and power, of love and goodness, a name that embodies for us a perfect supply for all our needs.

God is a Father, tender, and loving, and full of compassion, a God who, like a father, will be on our side against the whole universe. Our Lord could tell us emphatically not to be anxious or troubled about anything, for He knew His Father and knew that it was safe to trust Him utterly.

If we heap together all the best of all the fathers and mothers we have ever known or can imagine, that is a faint image of God, our Father in heaven.

In our Lord's last prayer in John 17, He says that He has declared to us the name of the Father so we may discover that the Father loves us as He loved His Son. What more can any soul want than to have a God whose name is "our Father," and whose character and ways must necessarily come up to the highest possibilities of His name?

All He asks of us is to let Him know when we need anything, and then leave the supplying of that need to Him; and He assures us that if we do this "the peace of God, which surpasses all understanding, will guard your hearts and minds through Christ Jesus" (Philippians 4:7).

The remedy for your discomfort and unrest is to be found in becoming acquainted with the Father.

"Peace I leave with you," [says our Lord,] "my peace I give to you.... Let not your heart be troubled, neither let it be afraid" (JOHN 14:27).

"*I am*

Among all the names of God perhaps the most comprehensive is Jehovah. The word Jehovah means the self-existing One, the "I am"; it is used as a direct revelation of what God is. In several places an explanatory word is added, revealing special characteristics.

Jehovah-jireh: "I am He who sees your need, and provides for it."

Jehovah-nissi: "I am your captain, your banner, He who will fight your battles for you."

Jehovah-shalom: "I am your peace. I have made peace for you, and My peace I give you."

your Captain"

If God is the one who provides, why, then, do I not have everything I want? you may ask. Only because God sees that what you want is not the thing you need, but probably exactly the opposite. Often, to give us what we need, the Lord is obliged to keep from us what we want.

If God is my captain, why then do I still come under enemy attack? Nothing is more abundantly proved in the Bible than that the Lord will fight for us if we will but let Him. He knows that we have no strength nor might against our spiritual enemies, and, He fights for us; and all He asks of us is to be still and let Him.

If God is my peace, why do I find myself in inner turmoil? Our idea of peace is that it must be outward before it can be inward, that all enemies must be driven away, and all troubles cease. But the Lord's idea was of an interior peace that could exist in the midst of turmoil, and could be triumphant over it. The ground of this sort of peace is found in the fact, not that we have overcome the world, but that Christ has overcome it. Only the conqueror can proclaim peace, and the people, whose battles He has fought, can do nothing but enter into it.

First give up all anxiety; and second, hand over your cares to God; and then stand steadfastly there; peace must come.

Be anxious for nothing, but in everything by prayer and supplication, with thanksgiving, let your requests be made known to God; and the peace of God, which surpasses all understanding, will guard your hearts and minds through Christ Jesus (PHILIPPIANS 4:6–7).

anxious for
nothing

Oh, taste and see that the Lord is good; blessed is the man who trusts in Him! Oh, fear the Lord, you His saints! There is no want to those who fear Him (PSALM 34:7–8).

Since God is omniscient, He must know what is the best and highest good of all; therefore His goodness must necessarily be beyond question. I can never express what this means to me. When I gained such a view of the goodness of God, I saw nothing could go wrong under His care, and it seemed to me that no one could ever be anxious again.

Over and over, when appearances have been against Him, and when I have been tempted to question whether He had been unkind, or neglectful, or indifferent, I have been brought up short by the words "The Lord is good"; and

The Lord is

I have seen that it is simply unthinkable that a God who is good could have done the bad things I had imagined.

The psalmist seemed to delight in repeating over and over again this blessed refrain, "for the Lord is good." And he exhorted everyone to join him in saying it. We must join our voices to His——The Lord is good——The Lord is good. But we must not say it with our lips only. We must "say" it with our whole being, with thought, word, and action, so that people will see we really mean it, and will be convinced that it is a tremendous fact.

The Lord is good, therefore all that He does must be good, no matter how it looks, and I can wait for His explanations.

good

You are God

Lord, You have been our dwelling place in all generations. Before the mountains were brought forth, or ever You had formed the earth and the world, even from everlasting to everlasting, You are God (PSALM 90:1–2).

Plagues in abundance may attack your body and your goods, but your body and your goods are not yourself; and nothing can come nigh you, the real interior you, while you are dwelling in God.

God

The comfort or discomfort of our outward lives depends more largely upon the dwelling place of our bodies than upon almost any other material thing; likewise, the comfort or discomfort of our inward life depends upon the dwelling place of our souls.

Our souls need a comfortable dwelling place, a comfort-filled home, even more than our bodies. When the Lord declares that He has been our dwelling place in all generations, the question remains, Are we living in our dwelling place? Our souls are made for God. He is our natural home, and we can never be at rest anywhere else.

When we read that God, who is our dwelling place, is also our fortress, it can mean only one thing, that if we will live in our dwelling place, we shall be safe and secure from every assault of every enemy that can attack us. "For in the time of trouble He shall hide me in His pavilion; in the secret place of His tabernacle He shall hide me; He shall set me high upon a rock" (Psalm 27:5).

is our fortress

We who are in this dwelling place shall be afraid of nothing; not for the terror by night, nor the arrow by day, nor for the pestilence that hides in darkness; thousands shall fall beside us and around us, but no evil shall befall the soul that is hidden in this divine dwelling place.

He who cares for the sparrows, and numbers the hairs of our head, cannot possibly fail us. He is an impregnable fortress. The moment I have really committed anything into this divine dwelling place, that moment all fear and anxiety should cease. While I keep anything in my own care, I may well fear and tremble, for it is indeed to the last degree unsafe; but in God's care, no security could be more absolute.

he practical thing to do, since God is our fortress and our high tower, is to surrender ourselves and all our interests into this divine dwelling place, and dismiss all care or anxiety about them from our minds.

SECTION THREE

A
Matter
of Faith

When I consider Your heavens, the work of Your fingers, the moon and the stars, which You have ordained, what is man that You are mindful of him, and the son of man that You visit him? For You have made him a little lower than the angels, and You have crowned him with glory and honor (PSALM 8:3–5).

consider

Your heavens...

When it comes to the comforts and blessings that God offers to His beloved children, He offers us more, much more, than we could ask or imagine. *Much more* is an expression used over and over in Scripture to tell us, if we would only believe it, that there is no need which any human being can ever know that cannot be much more met by the glorious salvation in Jesus Christ.

In the Sermon on the Mount, our Lord gives us the crowning "much more" of all. "Or what man is there among you who, if his son asks for bread, will give him a stone? Or if he asks for a fish, will he give him a serpent? If you then, being evil, know how to give good gifts to your children, how much more will your Father who is in heaven give good things to those who ask Him!" (Matthew 7:9–11).

In this we have a warrant for the supply of every need. Whatever our Father sees to be good for us is here abundantly promised. And the illustration used to convince us is one of universal application. In all ranks and conditions of life, among all nations—even in the hearts of birds and beasts—the parent's instinct never fails to provide for its offspring the best it can compass. Under no conditions of life will a parent, unless he is wicked beyond compare, give a stone when asked for bread, or a serpent when asked for fish. And could our God, who created the parent's heart, be worse than an earthly parent?

No, no, a thousand times no! What He will do is "much more," oh, so much more than even the tenderest mother could do. And if mothers and fathers "know how," as surely they do, to give good things to their children, "how much more" does He?

Let us resolve to lay aside every unbelief and out of the depths of our weakness and need assert a conquering faith in the mighty, "much more" grace of God.

What we must do is to shut the door resolutely and forever upon self and all of self's experiences, whether they be good or bad, and say with the psalmist, "I place my trust in You, o God."

Show

ℰXCERPTS FROM PSALM 16

Preserve me, O God, for in You I put my trust.

O Lord, You are the portion of my inheritance and my cup; You maintain my lot.

The lines have fallen to me in pleasant places; yes, I have a good inheritance.

I will bless the Lord who has given me counsel; my heart also instructs me in the night seasons.

I have set the Lord always before me; because He is at my right hand I shall not be moved.

Therefore my heart is glad, and my glory rejoices; my flesh also will rest in hope.

You will show me the path of life; in Your presence is fullness of joy; at Your right hand are pleasures forevermore.

me the path of life

Probably no subject connected with the life of faith has been so great an obstacle to spiritual growth and the cause of more discomfort than has the subject of self-examination. And yet it has been so constantly impressed upon us that it is our duty to examine ourselves, that the eyes of most of us are continually turned inward, and our gaze is fixed on our own interior states and feelings to such an extent that self, and not Christ, has come to fill the whole horizon.

It is a fact that we see what we look at, and cannot see what we look away from; and we cannot look to Jesus while we are looking at ourselves.

The power of victory and the power for endurance are to come from looking to Jesus and considering Him, not

from looking at or considering ourselves, or our circumstances, or our sins, or our temptations. Looking at ourselves causes weakness and defeat. The reason for this is
that when we look at ourselves, we see nothing but ourselves, and our own weakness, and poverty, and sin; we do
not and cannot see the remedy and the supply for these,
and as a matter of course we are defeated.

The remedy and the supply are there all the time, but
they are not to be found where we are looking, for they are
not in self but in Christ; and we cannot look at ourselves
and look at Christ at the same time.

Shall it be I or Christ? Shall I turn my back on Christ and look at myself, or shall I turn my back on self and look at Christ?

God is our rock and

Therefore we will not fear, even though the earth be removed, and though the mountains be carried into the midst of the sea; though its waters roar and be troubled, though the mountains shake with its swelling.... There is a river whose streams shall make glad the city of God...God is in the midst of her, she shall not be moved...(PSALM 46:2–5).

our foundation

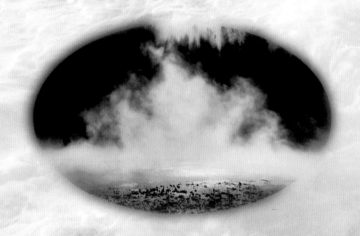

When everything in our lives and experience is shaken that can be shaken, and only that which cannot be shaken remains, we see that God only is our rock and our foundation, and we learn to have our expectation from Him alone.

Psalm 46:2–5 reads, "Therefore we will not fear, even though the earth be removed, and though the mountains be carried into the midst of the sea; though its waters roar and be troubled, though the mountains shake with its swelling....There is a river whose streams shall make glad the city of God ...God is in the midst of her, she shall not be moved; God shall help her, just at the break of dawn."

"Shall not be moved"—what an inspiring declaration! Can we, who are so easily moved by the things of earth, arrive at a place where nothing can upset our temper or disturb our calm? Yes.

The apostle Paul knew it. Everything in Paul's life and experience that could be shaken had been shaken, and he no longer counted his life, or any of life's possessions, dear to him. And we, if we will let God have His way with us, may come to the same place so that neither the little things of life, nor its great and heavy trials, can have power to move us from the peace that passes all understanding, which is the portion of those who rest only on God.

Our souls long for that kingdom that cannot be moved. And this kingdom may be our home, if we will submit to the shakings of God and learn to rest only and always on Him.

Therefore, my beloved brethren, be steadfast, immovable, always abounding in the work of the Lord, knowing that your labor is not in vain in the Lord

(1 CORINTHIANS 15:58).

God's salvation is not a purchase to be made, nor wages to be earned, nor a summit to be climbed, nor a task to be accomplished; it is a gift to be accepted, a gift that can only be accepted by faith.

Faith is a necessary element in the acceptance of any gift, whether earthly or heavenly. My friends may put their gifts on my table, or even place them in my lap, but unless I believe in their friendliness and honesty of purpose enough to accept these gifts, they can never become mine.

It is plain that the Bible is simply announcing, as it always does, the nature of things, when it declares that "according to your faith:" it shall be to you. And the sooner we

settle down to this the better. All our wavering comes from the fact that we do not believe in this law.

We acknowledge the Bible makes this broad promise, but we think it cannot mean what it says, that there must be additions to it. For instance, we add: "according to our fervency it shall be to us," or "according to our worthiness." So then our attention is directed to getting these matters settled, and we watch ourselves while overlooking the fundamental principle of faith, without which nothing can be done. We make the faithfulness of God, and the truth of His Word, depend on our feelings.

The person whose faith wavers is upset by the smallest trifles; the one whose faith is steadfast can look calmly at any circumstance.

"Be discouraged," says our lower nature, "for the world is a place of temptation and sin." "Be of good cheer," says Christ, "for I have overcome the world." There cannot be any room for discouragement in a world Christ has overcome.

Christ has overcome

Over and over the psalmist asks himself this question: "Why are you cast down, O my soul, and why are you disquieted within me?" And each time he answers himself with the argument of God: "Hope in God; for I shall yet praise him, who is the health of my countenance, and my God." He does not analyze his disquietude, or try to argue it away, but he turns at once to the Lord and by faith begins to praise Him.

It is the only way. Discouragement flies where faith appears; and, vice versa, faith flies when discouragement appears. We must choose between them, for they will not mix.

How different life would be if we looked upon discouragement in its true light, as a "speaking against God."

The battle
is the Lords

David said to the Philistine, "You come to me with a sword, with a spear, and with a javelin. But I come to you in the name of the Lord of hosts, the God of the armies of Israel, whom you have defied. This day the Lord will deliver you into my hand. ... Then all this assembly shall know that the Lord does not save with sword and spear; for the battle is the Lord's, and He will give you into our hands"

(1 SAMUEL 17:45–47).

David's fight with Goliath is an example of God's method of victory. The circumstances looked impossible from the human standpoint, but David had faith in His immovable God.

David's faith triumphed, and he shouted a shout of victory before even the battle had begun. David shouted before Goliath and all Israel, boldly proclaiming his confidence in a God who saves, a mighty God who commands unseen armies for whom the greatest giant is no match.

The secret of all successful warfare lies in this shout of faith. It is a secret incomprehensible to those who know nothing of the unseen divine power that waits on the demands of faith; a secret that must always seem, to those who do not understand it, the height of folly and imprudence.

And yet, see the results of such a faith: every word of David's triumphant shout of victory was fulfilled. So it will always be. Nothing can withstand the triumphant faith that links itself to omnipotence.

Do you know that God is for you, and that He will cause your enemies to turn back? If you do, then go out to meet your temptations, singing a song of triumph as you go.

SECTION FOUR

Thanksgiving or complaining—these words express two contrasting attitudes of the souls of God's children in regard to His dealings with them; and they are more powerful than we are inclined to believe in furthering or frustrating His purposes of comfort and peace toward us. The soul that complains can find comfort in nothing.

We cannot always give thanks for all things themselves, but we can always give thanks for God's love and care in the things that touch our lives. Not one thing can touch us except with His knowledge and permission. He is in them somewhere, and He is in them to compel, even the most grievous, to work together for our good and His glory.

It is not because things are good that we are to thank the Lord, but because He is good. We are not wise enough to judge as to things, whether they are really, in their essence, joys or sorrows. But we always know that the Lord is good, and that His goodness makes it absolutely certain that everything He provides or permits must be good; and must therefore be something for which we would be heartily thankful, if only we could see it with His eyes.

God invites us to enter His presence with thanksgiving and His courts with praise (Psalm 100). Could it be that giving thanks is the key that opens these gates more quickly than anything else?

In the
image of God

But we all, with unveiled face, beholding as in a mirror the glory of the Lord, are being transformed into the same image from glory to glory, just as by the Spirit of the Lord (2 CORINTHIANS 3:18).

God's ultimate purpose in our creation was that we should finally be transformed to the image of Christ. Christ is the pattern of what each of us is to be when finished. All the discipline and training of our lives is with this end in view; and God has implanted in every human heart a longing, however unformed and unexpressed, to reflect the glory of the Lord.

Paul also foreshadows this glorious consummation when he declares that if we suffer with Christ we shall also be glorified together with Him, and when he asserts that the "the sufferings of this present time are not worthy to be compared with the glory which shall be revealed in us" (Romans 8:18).

In view of such a glorious destiny, at which I dare not do more than hint, shall we not cheerfully welcome the processes, however painful they may be, by which we are to reach it? And shall we not strive eagerly and earnestly to be "laborers together with God" in helping to bring it about?

If we wish to be conformed to the image of Christ, we must live closer and ever closer to Him. We must become better acquainted with His character and His ways; we must look at things through His eyes, and judge all things by His standards.

I shall not

be moved

My soul, wait silently for God alone, for my expectation is from Him. He only is my rock and my salvation; He is my defense; I shall not be moved. In God is my salvation and my glory; the rock of my strength, and my refuge, is in God

(PSALM 62:5–7).

The last and greatest lesson the soul has to learn is the fact
that God, and God alone, is enough for all its needs. This is
the lesson that all His dealings with us are meant to teach;
and this is the crowning discovery of our whole Christian life.

God is enough!

If God is the "God of all comfort," as we have seen; if He is
our Shepherd; if He is really and truly our Father; if, in short,
all the many aspects we have been studying of His character

and His ways are actually true, then we must, it seems to me, come to the positive conviction that He is, in Himself alone, enough for all our possible needs, and that we may safely rest in Him absolutely and forever.

God is enough!

No soul can be really at rest until it has given up all dependence on everything else and has been forced to depend on the Lord alone.

is enough!

Beauty, Message, Ministry
Gift books from Moody

*I*n keeping with the Moody Press Vision Statement, the goal and purpose of our gift book line is to reach a wide audience with the gospel of Jesus Christ. We seek to put forth the biblical worldview in such a creative and powerful way that individuals worldwide will be inspired to live in increasing measure as fully devoted followers of Christ. Every gift book published by Moody Press will contain substantive material faithful to Scripture and a striking, creative design sure to attract a broad range of consumers.

Your Gift of Love is a beautifully-designed gift book containing key passages Gary Chapman's million-copy best-selling *The Five Love Languages*. To truly love our mates, we must understand how to communicate that love in the way they best receive it—in other words, we must learn their "love language." *Your Gift of Love* is an attractive gift book designed to not only express your love to your mate, but also to bless you both with a rich, enduring marriage. This book is also ideal for weddings, anniversaries, and other special occasions.